MATT RAWLE

Author of *The Redemption of Scrooge*

THE GRACE OF
Les Misérables

YOUTH STUDY BOOK

Josh Tinley

Abingdon Press/Nashville

The Grace of *Les Misérables*

Youth Study Book

978-1-5018-8721-5

19 20 21 22 23 24 25 26 27 28 — 10 9 8 7 6 5 4 3 2 1
MANUFACTURED IN THE UNITED STATES OF AMERICA

CONTENTS

Session 1

GRACE WELL RECEIVED

The Story of Jean Valjean

PLANNING THE SESSION

Through this session's discussion and activities, participants will be encouraged to

- reflect on moments of grace they've experienced.
- examine transformative moments in their lives.
- consider how relationships and promises give our lives purpose.
- confess their struggles and consider how they can learn and grow from their mistakes.

PREPARATION

- Read and reflect on the first chapter of Matt Rawle's *The Grace of Les Misérables*.
- Read through this Youth Study Book's session in its entirety to familiarize yourself with the material being covered.

- Read and reflect on the following Scriptures:

  ◊ Psalm 32:3-5
  ◊ Jeremiah 3:12-14
  ◊ Matthew 5:43-48
  ◊ Matthew 6:1-4
  ◊ Luke 6:32-36
  ◊ Luke 9:23-25
  ◊ James 5:15-16
  ◊ 1 John 1:8-10

- Make sure that you have a whiteboard or large sheet of paper on which you can record group members' ideas.
- Have a Bible, paper for taking notes, and a pen or pencil available for every participant.

OPENING ACTIVITY AND PRAYER (5 MINUTES)

Opening Activity

As participants arrive, welcome them to this study. Since the subject of this study is Victor Hugo's classic novel *Les Misérables*, and the many popular stage and screen versions of this story, open your time together with a discussion of your experiences with *Les Misérables*. Discuss some of the following questions:

- How familiar are you with *Les Misérables*?
- If you are familiar with *Les Misérables*, when did you first encounter it?
- What has stuck with you the most about this story?
- Why do you think Matt Rawle chose *Les Misérables* as the subject of a Bible study? What does this story have to teach Christians?

Opening Prayer

Lord, as we begin this study, we thank you for the witness of storytellers. We thank you for the story of Les Misérables, *for the ways it teaches us and challenges us, and for the questions that it raises. As we reflect on this story, may we also be mindful of your story and how we fit into it. Bless our time together that we can learn from Scripture, from story, and from one another. Amen.*

WATCH DVD SEGMENT (10 MINUTES)

STUDY AND DISCUSSION (35 MINUTES)

An Offering of Grace

Corresponds with "An Offering of Grace" in *The Grace of Les Misérables*, pages 19–22.

Read aloud or summarize for the group:

Rawle opens his book, appropriately, with grace. He points out that the story begins with grace. Jean Valjean, the story's protagonist, is struggling after serving a nineteen-year prison sentence for stealing bread to feed his sister's family (and for multiple escape attempts). Valjean, who is homeless, arrives at the church of Monseigneur Myriel. Myriel shows grace to Valjean. He welcomes him in, offers him a meal, and gives him a bed for the night. Unfortunately Valjean, who is desperate, steals Myriel's silverware and takes off in the middle of the night. Myriel, because he is so kind and welcoming, is better known by his nickname, M. Bienvenu.

Rawle relates the Monseigneur's grace to Jesus' teaching in Luke 6:32-36. Jesus teaches that there's nothing remarkable about showing love and generosity to friends and family. He commands us to show grace to all people, even our enemies. This often means making ourselves vulnerable. We don't know if the enemies and strangers we love will love us in return or even appreciate what we've done. By offering Jean Valjean a meal and a place to stay, Myriel was taking a risk. But he also was showing incredible faith in what was possible through God.

For discussion:

- Read Luke 6:32-36. What does Jesus teach about love in these verses?
- Who has shown you love and grace even though they didn't know you or you had done nothing to deserve it?
- Does the fact that Jean Valjean ran off with Myriel's silver mean that Myriel was foolish to give Valjean a meal and a place to stay? Why, or why not?

- What risks do we take when we show love and grace to enemies and strangers?
- Why, do you think, does Jesus call us to love our enemies, even if doing so is sometimes dangerous?

A Changed Life

Corresponds with "A Changed Life" in *The Grace of Les Misérables*, pages 23–26.

Read aloud or summarize for the group:

Soon after Jean Valjean runs off with the stolen silver, the local police apprehend him and take him back to the church. Instead of identifying Valjean as a thief, M. Bienvenu tells the officer that the silver had been a gift. He even claims that Valjean had forgotten to take additional silver pieces, candlesticks. M. Bienvenu tells Valjean to take this gift and use it to become an honest man.

Rawle points out that this gift of grace from M. Bienvenu is a turning point in Jean Valjean's life, a convicting moment. This doesn't mean that everything immediately changes for Valjean or that he doesn't have additional struggles or lapses in judgment. But M. Bienvenu's gift changed Valjean's worldview. It gave him a desire to change and hope for the future.

Scripture tells about many of these conversion moments. One of the most famous is the conversion of Saul (better known as Paul). Saul, an enemy of the church, had an experience of the risen Christ on his way to arrest Christians in Damascus. This experience gives Saul a new purpose. Instead of persecuting Christians, he becomes a leader of the church and a missionary throughout the Roman world. Moments of grace reorient our lives and set us on a new path.

For discussion:

- When M. Bienvenu told the police that the silver had been a gift to Jean Valjean, he wasn't being truthful. Was what M. Bienvenu did justified? Why, or why not?
- When has someone shown you incredible love and grace, even when you didn't deserve it? How did these experiences shape and change your life?

- What did these people risk by showing you grace?
- What other turning-point or convicting moments have you had in your life?
- How have these moments affected how you see the world and your purpose in life?

Discipline and Responsibility

Corresponds with "Discipline and Responsibility" in *The Grace of Les Misérables*, pages 26–31.

Read aloud or summarize for the group:

In response to M. Bienvenu's grace and the hope of a new life, Jean Valjean tears up his yellow ticket, which identifies him as a criminal out on parole. Then the story skips ahead several years. We don't know exactly what happens to Valjean during these years, but he ends up becoming a well-to-do factory owner and mayor of the town of Montreuil. When Valjean, who is now known as M. Madeleine, heroically saves a man trapped under a cart, the police chief, Javert (who had been Valjean's prison guard years earlier) recognizes him as the criminal who'd broken his parole.

Before Javert arrests M. Madeleine, police arrest another man with a similar description whom they believe to be Valjean. Madeleine, the real Valjean, can keep his secret and let the other man take the fall. Or he can be honest and risk being arrested and returned to prison. After spending a night agonizing over his decision, Valjean decides to turn himself in.

Rawle points out that Valjean sincerely wants to be a good person but keeps running into obstacles that make living a good life difficult. As Christians, we should be able to sympathize. We know that we are redeemed by God's grace through Christ, but we often find that following Christ's teaching and example is a daily struggle.

For discussion:

- Jean Valjean in *Les Misérables* has spent most of his adult life being punished severely for small crimes. If he were caught violating his parole, he could have been jailed, destroying the new life he'd built for himself. Would Jean Valjean have been justified not fessing up? Why, or why not? Would he have been justified letting someone else take the blame?

- When have you been afraid to be honest or to take accountability for your actions?
- Read Luke 9:23-25. What does Jesus mean when he commands his followers to "take up their cross"? What does it mean to do this "daily"?
- In the story of *Les Misérables*, how is Jean Valjean tempted to gain the world by losing his soul?
- What temptations make it difficult for you to take up your cross daily and be a faithful follower of Christ?

A Salvation of Secrets

Corresponds with "A Salvation of Secrets" in *The Grace of Les Misérables*, pages 31–35.

Read aloud or summarize for the group:

When Jean Valjean confesses, he is allowed to leave freely. But Javert, the police chief, is right behind him. Meanwhile, we meet Fantine, a young woman who was fired from Valjean's factory. Valjean learns that Fantine is in poor health and vows to her that he will find her daughter, Cosette, and care for her. Soon after Valjean makes this promise, Javert finds and arrests him. But Valjean escapes from prison and sets off to find Cosette.

Jean Valjean devotes himself entirely to finding and raising Cosette. When he finds her, in the care of a shady innkeeper, he and Cosette set off for a new life in Paris. On the run from Javert in the cold of winter, Valjean is desperate. In a bit of good fortune, he runs into a man named Fauchelevent, whose life he had saved back in Montreuil. Fauchelevent takes in Valjean and Cosette and agrees to keep their identities secret.

Rawle points out that Valjean's promise to Fantine changes him. His devotion to this vow gives Valjean's life meaning and shows him what it means to love. Our devotion to Christ has a similar effect on us. Love becomes our way of life and our purpose for living. Traditionally the season of Lent is a time to focus on spiritual disciplines such as prayer, Scripture reading, fasting, and service that draw us closer to Jesus and constantly remind us that we are followers of Christ.

For discussion:

- Because of his promise to Fantine, Jean Valjean goes on a mission to find and care for Cosette. When have you been on a mission? When have you been fully devoted to a certain task? What made this task so important?
- What relationships have given you a new outlook on life? What relationships have challenged you to live differently?
- What spiritual practices or disciplines do you practice regularly?
- What disciplines or practices have you taken during the Lenten season (or for another special time of year)?
- How do regular habits of prayer, worship, Bible study, and service keep us focused? How do they give us purpose?

Confession and Honesty

Corresponds with "Confession and Honesty" in *The Grace of Les Misérables*, pages 35–39.

Read aloud or summarize for the group:

Skipping ahead, one of the most important relationships in *Les Misérables* is the relationship between Jean Valjean and Marius, a young man who falls in love with Cosette. Marius is injured in the 1832 Paris uprising. Valjean, who worries that Marius will take away his adopted daughter, considers leaving him to die but instead commits to saving the young man's life. This requires Valjean to drag Marius through the Paris sewers.

Carrying a dying man through the sewers is an unforgiving task. At one point the sewage is deep enough to drown someone. But Valjean and Marius eventually make it to safety. Marius regains his health and plans to marry Cosette. To avoid signing the wedding papers using a false name, Valjean presents an injured hand in a sling. However, he finally reveals his true identity and confesses the crimes he's committed. This causes a rift between Valjean and Marius that lasts until Marius discovers that Valjean was the one who had saved his life. The story ends with forgiveness and reconciliation, and Valjean dies in peace.

Rawle notes that, even years after Valjean found hope and love and purpose in his promise to Fantine, there are still times when he finds himself in total darkness. This is true for all of us. Christ offers us redemption and the hope of eternal life, but he doesn't promise that our lives will be free from pain and suffering. We just know that the pain and suffering don't get the last word. Christ gets the last word.

For discussion:

- Valjean saved Marius's life, even though he didn't really like Marius and didn't get credit for what he did. Read Matthew 5:43-48 and 6:1-4. What does Jesus teach about our attitude when it comes to doing good?
- Even after finding purpose, Valjean was tested many times. What struggles and obstacles have challenged your faith?
- How do you find hope in times of darkness?
- Why is it important that we confess our sins and struggles? To whom do you feel comfortable confessing?
- When have you had to make an uncomfortable confession?

Activity: Petty Confessions

Supplies: Bibles, note cards or slips of paper, pens or pencils

Hand out note cards or slips of paper. Each person should write on his or her card or slip confessions to two small crimes. A small crime might be sticking gum under desks when they were in school or carving their initials into a public bench. These should be things that are definitely wrong but that probably don't cause a lot of lingering guilt. One of these confessions should be true, the other should be completely made up.

Allow everyone a few minutes to work. Then have each person read aloud both of their confessions. The rest of the group should guess which of the two confessions is true and which is false.

Read aloud or summarize the following:

Confession is a recurring theme in *Les Misérables*. Jean Valjean confesses crimes to the authorities, confesses his identity and wrongdoings to Marius, and confesses his true feelings to himself and those he cares about.

Read the following Scriptures about confession. For each one, discuss what it means for us as followers of Christ.

- Psalm 32:3-5
- Jeremiah 3:12-14
- James 5:15-16
- 1 John 1:8-10

Activity: *Turning Points*

When M. Bienvenu gave Jean Valjean a meal and place to stay, covered for him when he was caught stealing, and gave him silver as a gift, Valjean experienced a turning point. His life was forever changed.

Invite participants to reflect on turning points in their lives. After everyone has had a minute to reflect in silence, divide participants into teams of three or four. In teams, participants should discuss the following questions about their turning points:

- What was your turning point? Why was this moment significant?
- How did your life change as a result of this moment? How was your life different before this turning point than it was afterward?
- What didn't change as a result of this moment? How was your life still the same?

Come back together as a group. A volunteer should read aloud 2 Corinthians 5:16-17. Discuss:

- What does it mean to be a "new creation" in Christ?
- What does it mean that we won't recognize people by "human standards"?
- How have you been changed as a result of your relationship in Christ?

CLOSING ACTIVITY AND PRAYER (10 MINUTES)

Closing Activity

Title a large sheet of paper, "What Christians can learn from Jean Valjean's story." To close your time together, have each person list on the large sheet of paper one thing that he or she has learned about his or her faith from this session. Invite participants to explain what they wrote.

Closing Prayer

God of new life and new creation, thank you for the stories that teach us about love and grace and what it means to be made new. Open our eyes, ears, and minds to how you are working to redeem and transform all people. Thank you also for this time we've had to learn from one another and grow together in faith. We pray all these things in Jesus' name. Amen.

Session 2

WHEN GRACE AND JUSTICE COLLIDE

The Story of Javert

PLANNING THE SESSION

Through this session's discussion and activities, participants will be encouraged to

- reflect on how our pursuits and obsessions can become unhealthy and warp our priorities.
- examine the rules and laws we follow and how, by focusing on the letter of the law, we sometimes miss the true meaning of the law.
- discuss the disguises we wear around certain groups of people and why we hide from our true selves.
- consider how our relationships, rather than strict interpretations of the law, should govern how we live.

PREPARATION

- Read and reflect on the second chapter of Matt Rawle's *The Grace of Les Misérables*.

- Read through this Youth Study Book's session in its entirety to familiarize yourself with the material being covered.
- Read and reflect on the following Scriptures:

  ◊ 1 Samuel 28:3-19
  ◊ Matthew 5:21-30
  ◊ Matthew 5:33-37
  ◊ Matthew 5:38-42
  ◊ Matthew 20:1-16
  ◊ Matthew 22:34-40
  ◊ Mark 2:23-28
  ◊ Mark 3:1-6
  ◊ Luke 16:1-9
  ◊ Luke 18:18-23

- Make sure that you have a whiteboard or large sheet of paper on which you can record group members' ideas.
- Have a Bible, paper for taking notes, and a pen or pencil available for every participant.

Opening Activity and Prayer (5 minutes)

Opening Activity

As participants arrive, welcome them to this study. Since this session will focus on Javert, the antagonist in *Les Misérables*, open your time together with a discussion of your favorite fictional villains:

- Which villains (from books, movies, television, comics, theater, and so forth) do you find most intimidating?
- Which villains do you find most interesting? Why?
- What makes a character an interesting or effective villain?
- What are some examples of villains who find redemption? What can we learn from their stories?

Opening Prayer

Lord, as we continue this study, we thank you for the gift of grace. We thank you for the story of Les Misérables, *and for the questions it raises about grace and justice. Bless our time together that we can learn from Scripture, from story, and from one another. Amen.*

WATCH DVD SEGMENT (10 MINUTES)

STUDY AND DISCUSSION (35 MINUTES)

By the Letter, Not the Spirit

Corresponds with "By the Letter, Not the Spirit" in *The Grace of Les Misérables*, pages 43–46.

Read aloud or summarize for the group:

On the surface, Javert seems to be the villain in *Les Misérables*. He spends much of the story tracking down Jean Valjean and making his life difficult. While Javert is definitely the antagonist, Rawle suggests that we shouldn't think of him as a villain. Javert is devoted to law and order. He cares about rules and follows them to a T. For Javert, flexibility and compromise are not part of the job.

Order has its place. Scripture begins with God bringing order to chaos. Order is necessary to keep people safe, and it is responsible for efficiency and productivity in the workplace. Early in *Les Misérables* Javert works as a prison warden; he maintains order to prevent chaos. He takes this mindset into his work as a police officer and his pursuit of Jean Valjean. But, at times, Javert's devotion to upholding the law causes him to lose sight of the spirit of the law.

Rawle points out that Javert's attitude is similar to that of some of the Pharisees whom Jesus encountered. Pharisees were known for righteousness and strictly following Jewish law. In Mark 3, some Pharisees confront Jesus when they see his disciples picking grain on the Sabbath. According to the law, people should rest from any work on the Sabbath. But, Jesus explained, the Pharisees had missed the point of the Sabbath laws. The Sabbath was a gift from

God. If people were forbidden from gathering food to meet their basic needs or to feed the hungry, the Sabbath would feel like more of a punishment.

Jesus teaches us to honor and follow the law but also to consider the purpose behind these laws. If following the law doesn't draw us into a closer relationship with God or provide an abundant life for God's people, we're probably missing the point.

For discussion:

- Why is order, and the rule of law, so important?
- What are some laws and rules that don't make much sense to you? Why, do you think, are these rules in place?
- When have you been so focused on the letter of the law that you lost sight of the meaning behind the law?
- Read Mark 2:23-28. How do the Pharisees in these verses miss the point of the Sabbath laws?
- Read Matthew 22:34-40. According to Jesus, the entire law is based on which two commandments? What does this tell us about the purpose of the law?

Searching

Corresponds with "Searching" in *The Grace of Les Misérables*, pages 47–50.

Read aloud or summarize for the group:

Javert's encounters with Jean Valjean early in *Les Misérables* leave him obsessed. He makes tracking down Valjean his life's work. Rawle writes, "For Inspector Javert, everything points to Jean Valjean. Every crime and every criminal seems to be linked to the escaped convict, which only leads Javert into a deeper obsession to find him."

We all probably know someone who has become obsessed with a single goal or pursuit. Maybe we've been in this situation ourselves. In some cases, this singular devotion leads to greatness. Many of our culture's best artists, athletes, and professionals achieved their status by obsessing over their craft. But being so devoted to one thing also can warp our priorities and cloud our judgment. Javert is so infatuated with arresting Jean Valjean that he doesn't stop to consider whether this is a good idea.

Throughout his ministry Jesus challenged people's assumptions about the way things work. He told a story where the hero was not a holy religious leader but a Samaritan—part of a group that many faithful Jewish people considered the enemy. He told another story where a father welcomed with open arms a son who'd betrayed and dishonored him. Jesus warned his followers, along with some hostile religious leaders, not to be so obsessed with the letter of the law that they missed the point of the law.

For discussion:

- Whom do you know who is obsessed with a particular activity, discipline, profession, or way of life? Have you ever been obsessed with one thing?
- What are the benefits to having an obsessive devotion to one thing?
- What are the drawbacks to being solely devoted to one thing?
- Read Matthew 5:21-30. How does Jesus challenge people's assumptions?
- Why, do you think, did religious leaders who were obsessed with following the law grow so frustrated with Jesus?

In Disguise

Corresponds with "In Disguise" in *The Grace of Les Misérables*, pages 50–53.

Read aloud or summarize for the group:

You would think that Javert, who is obsessed with law and order, would be a man of integrity. But as Javert gets desperate in his pursuit of Jean Valjean, he turns to deception. He disguises himself as a beggar, hoping that Valjean will reveal himself through his generosity. Javert's ruse is almost successful in catching Valjean, but it also represents a turning point. Javert fails to demonstrate the honor he demands from others.

We encounter a similar story in Scripture. Saul, the first king of Israel, has outlawed witches and magicians. But when Israel is threatened by the Philistine army and none of Saul's prophets are giving him the answers he wants, he puts on a disguise and goes looking for a witch. He finds a witch who summons the spirit of the late, great prophet Samuel. Instead of offering the king advice or military strategy, Samuel predicts that Saul and his entire army will die in battle the next day. This is exactly what happens.

Most of us know what it's like to wear a disguise. Even if we've never gone fully incognito, we may have hidden parts of our personality around certain people. Or we might pretend to have certain skills, interests, or experiences to impress someone. Maybe we have even convinced ourselves to like a particular style of music, fashion, or movies to fit in better with a group we want to be a part of. Sometimes our disguises are harmless. But too often they cause us to lose sight of who we are and what we value.

For discussion:

- What disguises have you worn? How have you changed your identity or personality around certain people?
- Read 1 Samuel 28:3-19. Why does King Saul disguise himself? How does his plan backfire?
- Javert puts on a disguise when he is desperate and running out of ideas. What sorts of situations might cause you to conceal your identity or pretend to be someone you aren't?
- When, if ever, can putting on a disguise be beneficial?
- How can wearing disguises be destructive?

Deception

Corresponds with "Deception" in *The Grace of Les Misérables*, pages 53–56.

Read aloud or summarize for the group:

When Javert disguises himself to catch Valjean, we see him as dishonorable and deceptive. But Valjean, the hero of the story, spends much of the story living under a false name. And Valjean's transformation begins when a priest, M. Bienvenu, tells a fib about giving Valjean the silver. We don't judge Valjean or M. Bienvenu nearly as harshly as we judge Javert.

Jesus tells a parable about a manager who is fired for mismanaging his master's property. Facing an uncertain future, the manager goes to each of his master's debtors and (without his master's permission) cuts each debt significantly. He did this so that people would "welcome [him] into their houses." Instead of punishing the manager for being dishonest, the master actually commends him for being so clever. It's a weird story. Why is the master so understanding of his manager's dishonesty?

One possibility is that the master is impressed that the manager values relationships over money. Jesus follows the parable by making a distinction between worldly riches and true wealth. The choices we make are not just about the rules we follow but about what we value.

For discussion:

- Read Jesus' parable of the dishonest manager in Luke 16:1-9. What, do you think, is the purpose of this story?
- When, if ever, is dishonesty justified?
- When might strictly following the rules have a negative effect on our relationships?

The Rejection of Grace

Corresponds with "The Rejection of Grace" in *The Grace of Les Misérables*, pages 57–60.

Read aloud or summarize for the group:

Javert's parents were criminals. He was born and spent his formative years in a prison. But his experiences give him no sympathy for criminals and prisoners. Rather, his devotion to upholding the law is his way of distancing himself from his criminal past. He has no tolerance or grace for lawbreakers.

During the 1832 Paris uprising, Javert works as a spy. He infiltrates a group of student revolutionaries in hopes of bringing them to justice. When the students learn that Javert is a spy and realize that their revolution will end in defeat, the leader of the rebels orders Javert to be executed. While Javert is bound and awaiting execution, Jean Valjean—the man whom Javert has pursued and tortured for years—cuts the disgraced officer's restraints and sets him free.

Javert cannot handle this gift of grace. He demands that Valjean take revenge, but Valjean refuses. Toward the end of the story, after Valjean has dragged Marius through the sewers to rescue him, Javert meets Valjean at the sewer's exit. Valjean assumes that his old nemesis will finally arrest him, but Javert cannot. Arresting the man who'd saved his life would be dishonorable. On the other hand, letting Valjean go would contradict everything Javert believed in and lived for. Conflicted, Javert jumps from the parapet of a bridge and takes his own life.

For discussion:

- Javert has a very rigid worldview, which he refuses to change. What experiences have caused you to change your worldview? How did your outlook on life change as a result of these experiences?
- How does it feel when someone treats you with love and grace even though you've done nothing to deserve it?
- How does it feel when someone treats you with love and grace even though you've treated that person badly?
- Read Matthew 20:1-16. Why are the workers who started at the beginning of the day so upset? Are they right to be angry?
- What does this parable teach us about grace and justice?

Activity: Don't Break Your Concentration

Supplies: any supplies necessary for the task you choose (see below).

Have a volunteer focus on doing a rote or repetitive task. Examples would be bouncing a ping-pong ball on a paddle, saying the prime numbers in order starting with "2," or continually going through the alphabet backwards. While this person performs this task, everyone else should try to distract him or her and break his or her concentration. Those who are breaking concentration should not touch the person or anything he or she is using (such as the ball or paddle).

See how long the person can continue doing the assigned task before he or she breaks. If time permits, redo this activity with different people.

Then discuss:

- What activities or interests have you been so devoted to that nothing could break your focus?
- How did focusing solely on one thing affect your view of the world, your outlook on life, and your priorities? What were the positive effects of your obsession? What were the negative effects?
- When has a distraction been a blessing? How did it reorient your life or priorities?
- How, do you think, does God work through distractions?

Activity: But I Say . . .

Supplies: Bibles, paper, and pens or pencils

Jesus frequently challenged people's readings and interpretations of the law. He challenges us to get past the letter of the law and to focus instead on the spirit of the law.

Read aloud the Scriptures below. For each one, discuss the difference between the letter of the law and the spirit of the law.

- Matthew 5:21-24
- Matthew 5:33-37
- Matthew 5:38-42
- Mark 3:1-6
- Luke 18:18-23

Then divide into pairs or teams of three. Each pair or team should write a short paragraph that challenges people to go beyond the letter of a current-day law or rule. For example:

> You have heard that the neighborhood noise ordinance says, "No loud noises after 11:00 p.m." But I say, "A lot of people have work and school early in the morning, so keep it down starting at 8:30 during the week."

Invite each pair or team to read aloud their paragraphs. Then discuss:

- What can we learn from these Scriptures, and our paragraphs, about what Jesus expects from us?

CLOSING ACTIVITY AND PRAYER (10 MINUTES)

Closing Activity

Title a large sheet of paper, "What Christians can learn from Javert's story." To close your time together, have each person list on the large sheet of paper one thing that he or she has learned about his or her faith from this session. Invite participants to explain what they wrote.

Closing Prayer

God of new life and new creation, thank you for the stories that teach us about our priorities and about how we approach your laws. Open our eyes, ears, and minds to how we can get past the literal meaning of the rules and laws we follow and focus instead on living as your people. Thank you also for this time we've had to learn from one another and grow together in faith. We pray all these things in Jesus' name. Amen.

Session 3

THE POOR ARE ALWAYS WITH YOU

The Story of Fantine

PLANNING THE SESSION

Through this session's discussion and activities, participants will be encouraged to

- consider the responsibility we have toward people who are suffering and struggling.
- examine how we can find hope and optimism during times of despair.
- reflect on what it means to "reap" what we "sow."
- confess ways we have failed to show love and compassion toward those who are hurting.

PREPARATION

- Read and reflect on the third chapter of Matt Rawle's *The Grace of Les Misérables*.

- Read through this Youth Study Book's session in its entirety to familiarize yourself with the material being covered.
- Read and reflect on the following Scriptures:

  ◊ Matthew 25:31-46
  ◊ Romans 5:1-5
  ◊ Romans 8:26-28
  ◊ Galatians 6:7
  ◊ Colossians 3:12-14

- Make sure that you have a whiteboard or large sheet of paper on which you can record group members' ideas.
- Have a Bible, paper for taking notes, and a pen or pencil available for every participant.

OPENING ACTIVITY AND PRAYER (5 MINUTES)

Opening Activity

As participants arrive, welcome them to this study. This session will focus on several important characters, including Fantine, a poor factory worker who goes to great lengths to give her daughter, Cosette, a chance at a better life. In honor of Fantine, discuss:

- What sacrifices have people made on your behalf so that you would have a better life?

List these ideas on a whiteboard or large sheet of paper.

- How would your life have been different without these people making these sacrifices?

Opening Prayer

Lord, as we continue this study, we thank you for the gift of grace. We thank you for the story of Les Misérables, *and for the questions it raises about survival and caring for the poor. Bless our time together that we can learn from Scripture, from story, and from one another. Amen.*

WATCH DVD SEGMENT (10 MINUTES)

STUDY AND DISCUSSION (35 MINUTES)

When Dreams Become Nightmares

Corresponds with "When Dreams Become Nightmares" in *The Grace of Les Misérables*, pages 62–66.

Read aloud or summarize for the group:

Fantine in *Les Misérables* is a young single mother who moves to Montreuil to find work. She seeks lodging at Thénardier's inn and asks Thénardier and his wife if they can watch her daughter, Cosette, until she can find work and permanent housing. Entrusting Cosette to strangers is a dangerous, desperate move, but Fantine will do whatever it takes to give her daughter a chance.

Fantine finds work in Jean Valjean's factory. Thénardier, pretending that Cosette is ill, demands more money from Fantine. Making matters worse, Fantine loses her factory job when it is revealed that she has a child. She falls deep into debt and must resort to even more extreme measures. Fantine sells her hair and sells her teeth, then becomes a prostitute.

Les Misérables means, literally, "the miserable ones." Fantine is one of these miserable ones. She is abused and exploited and eventually dies in poverty. The people of Montreuil failed her. But, as we discover later in the story, her efforts to create a better life for Cosette are not in vain.

For discussion:

- Look back on your list from the opening activity. What risks did these people take to improve your life?
- Based on your knowledge of *Les Misérables*, how did the people of Montreuil fail Fantine?
- Read Matthew 25:31-46. What does Jesus teach us about loving and serving him?
- Who are the "least of these" in our community? Who is overlooked and neglected?

- How does our congregation serve people who are overlooked and neglected in our community?
- What more could we do to serve these people?

Survival of the Fittest

Corresponds with "Survival of the Fittest" in *The Grace of Les Misérables*, pages 66–71.

Read aloud or summarize for the group:

When we first meet Thénardier, the innkeeper, he comes off as respectable and compassionate—the type of person whom Fantine could trust with her child. But the more we get to know Thénardier, the less respectable and compassionate he seems. He cheats the patrons of the bar, extorts money from Fantine, and abuses Cosette.

Cosette, Fantine's young daughter, lives in a constant state of fear. While Eponine, Thénardier's own daughter, lives in luxury, Cosette is treated with scorn. On Christmas Eve night, Mme. Thénardier sends her out in the dark to fetch more water for the guests at the inn. Cosette has an intense fear of the dark.

Being afraid of the dark is a common fear. Fear of the dark is a fear of the unknown and a fear of being alone. And figurative darkness can be just as frightening as literal darkness. When we can't see what the future holds or how we'll get through the next week, we lose hope. The good news is that God seeks us out in times of darkness. God speaks to us through the presence and encouragement of other people, through feelings of assurance, and by putting new opportunities in front of us. For Cosette, God was present in the person of Jean Valjean, who finds her when she is out fetching water and eventually takes her in as his adopted daughter.

For discussion:

- Why, do you think, is fear of the dark such a common fear?
- How has God spoken to you and comforted you in times of darkness and uncertainty?
- How has God reached out to you through other people to give you hope?

- Read Psalm 139:4-12. What do these verses tell us about God and times of darkness?

You Reap What You Sow?

Corresponds with "You Reap What You Sow?" in *The Grace of Les Misérables*, pages 71–74.

Read aloud or summarize for the group:

Galatians 6:7 says, "Make no mistake, God is not mocked. A person will harvest what they plant." A more common translation is, "You reap what you sow." In other words, you get what you deserve.

This sentiment sounds good on the surface. But is it accurate? Thénardier in *Les Misérables* is, by all appearances, a nasty person. He takes advantage of the vulnerable and abuses the young girl in his care. Yet, he prospers. By the end of the musical version of the story he and his family are among the French elite. Where is the justice? Why doesn't his family get what they deserve? (In the original novel, Thénardier loses his inn and goes bankrupt.)

Meanwhile, Jean Valjean can't seem to shake his past. No matter what he does to reform himself or to become a contributing member of society, he is still considered a criminal in the eyes of the law. But Valjean is able to find peace toward the end of his life, in part thanks to Thénardier, who inadvertently reveals to Marius that Valjean was the one who saved his life. Because of this, Valjean, Cosette, and Marius are able to find peace as a family. When he's dying at the end of the story, Valjean—in the musical version of *Les Misérables*—sings the line, "To love another person is to see the face of God." What Valjean finds is far more valuable than any of the temporary luxuries that Thénardier enjoys.

For discussion:

- What does the phrase, "You reap whatever you sow" (Galatians 6:7 NRSV), mean to you? How do you see truth in this saying? When, if ever, does this saying fall short?
- How do you respond when someone you think of as an evil person prospers? How *should* you respond?
- Read Romans 8:26-28. What do these verses say to people, such as

the protagonists of *Les Misérables*, who find themselves in dire and desperate circumstances?
- How has God helped your weaknesses?
- Why, do you think, are we so tempted by temporary riches instead of greater things such as faith, love, and hope?

The Pure in Heart

Corresponds with "The Pure in Heart" in *The Grace of Les Misérables*, pages 74–77.

Read aloud or summarize for the group:

The name Gavroche has become synonymous with "street urchin." Gavroche, one of the miserable ones in *Les Mis*, is an orphan who lives on the streets and does what he can to get by. He is a thief, but he doesn't steal out of greed or spite but to survive. (In the novel, he is the unwanted son of the Thénardiers.)

Gavroche is small in stature. But he makes up for what he lacks in size and wealth with spirit. He is lovable and tenderhearted while also being persistent and tenacious. His optimism and will to survive give hope to others who struggle and suffer on the streets.

Early on, Gavroche brightens the dreary mood of *Les Misérables*. But later in the story, he plays a key role in the 1832 Paris uprising. He is the one who reveals that Javert is a spy. By doing so, he saves the lives of many rebels. During the fighting he sneaks through the barricade to gather more ammunition for the rebels, who are running out of supplies. In this act of bravery, he is shot and killed.

Rawle points out that Gavroche, the street child who is ignored by so many, defies expectations. He is a sign of hope despite living a life of despair and desperation. He is able to give so much despite having so little.

For discussion:

- Whom do you know who, like Gavroche, is a symbol of hope and optimism?
- Whom do you know who has defied expectations and has accomplished things that few thought they were capable of?

- Read Romans 5:1-5. What do these verses tell us about hope in times of despair and desperation?
- What gives you hope and optimism during difficult times?
- Whom do you know who is persistent and tenacious?
- How do you find the strength and energy to persevere in trying times?

Offering Yourself

Corresponds with "Offering Yourself" in *The Grace of Les Misérables*, pages 78–81.

Read aloud or summarize for the group:

Many of the young characters in *Les Misérables* live unpleasant lives. Eponine is an exception. She is the eldest daughter in the Thénardier family, and her parents cater to her every whim (something they don't do for any of the other children in their care). Early in the story Eponine feels contempt and disgust toward Cosette, the factory worker's child whom her parents are being paid to care for.

Eponine's perfect life doesn't last. Her family faces financial hardship, and she gets a taste of what life is like for those whom she felt were below her. After time passes and we see her as a young woman, Eponine is living in Paris and struggling to get by, like the other miserable ones. Meanwhile, Cosette, through her adoptive father, becomes affluent and lives comfortably. With roles reversed, Eponine learns selflessness and compassion.

Both Eponine and Cosette fall for Marius. Marius loves Cosette. Eponine is sad that her love is unrequited, but she is not resentful. Eponine loves Marius to the end. During the Paris uprising, she shields him from a soldier's bullet, sacrificing her life to save his.

For discussion:

- What life experiences have caused you to be more compassionate and empathetic?
- What would you say to your younger self about how you treat and show empathy to other people?

- Read Colossians 3:12-14. Whom do you know who exemplifies the qualities Paul talks about in these verses?
- What factors might make you jealous, resentful, or spiteful toward someone else? How can you overcome these urges and instead show kindness and compassion?
- What risks have you taken for the good of someone else? When have you been unwilling to take a risk or make a sacrifice for someone else?

Activity: *You Have Done It for Me*

Supplies: Bibles, a whiteboard or large sheet of paper, and markers

Read aloud Matthew 25:31-40. In Jesus' description of the judgment of the nations, he teaches us that when we show compassion to the "least of these," we show compassion to him.

List in one column on a whiteboard or large sheet of paper the people whom Jesus names in these verses. (Leave space between each group you list.) Then to the right of each group on your list, identify ways you can serve those people in your community, or elsewhere in the world, today.

(Those who are "thirsty" might include people who don't have access to clean drinking water. The "naked" includes both people who literally lack clothing and those who are vulnerable and unsafe in other ways.)

Discuss:

- What opportunities do you have every day do help out the people on our list?
- How do we serve Jesus by serving those who are hungry, sick, vulnerable, and alone?
- What reasons do you give to not help the "least of these"?
- How can you be more intentional about showing love to people who are desperate and hurting? How can you make compassion part of your daily routine?

Activity: *Trouble, Endurance, Character, Hope*

Supplies: Bibles, paper, and pens or pencils

Read aloud Romans 5:1-5. In these verses the apostle Paul explains that "trouble produces endurance, endurance produces character, and character produces hope."

With this in mind, each person should create a simple flow chart drawing either from personal experience or from a fictional story they are familiar with. The instructions are below:

- This chart should begin with a box labeled, "Trouble." Write in this box about a troubling experience (either personal or fictional).
- Draw an arrow from the "Trouble" box to one labeled, "Endurance." Write in this box about how you, or the fictional character, were able to persist through the trouble you described.
- From "Endurance," draw an arrow to a box labeled, "Character." Write in this box, how enduring trouble made you, or the fictional character, a better person.
- Finally, draw an arrow from "Character" to a box labeled, "Hope." Describe in this box how the experiences in the other three boxes provide hope, either to you or the fictional character or to other people whose lives you affect.

After everyone has had time to make a chart, invite volunteers to summarize what they wrote.

Discuss:

- How does this activity relate to the characters we've discussed from *Les Misérables*? How do their troubling experiences produce endurance, character, and hope?
- What do these verses say about how we should approach pain, suffering, and despair?

Note: While God is present with us during trying times and walks with us as we learn and grow from these experiences, we should not think of suffering as part of God's plan. God does not hurt us so that we'll have character and hope. Rather, pain and suffering are an inevitable part of living in a broken and sinful world. God works through us to heal this pain.

CLOSING ACTIVITY AND PRAYER (10 MINUTES)

Closing Activity

Title a large sheet of paper, "What Christians can learn from the stories of Fantine, Cosette, Gavroche, and Eponine." To close your time together, have each person list on the large sheet of paper one thing that he or she has learned about his or her faith from this session. Invite participants to explain what they wrote.

Closing Prayer

God of endurance, character, and hope, thank you for the stories that teach us about empathy and compassion. Open our eyes, ears, and minds to the needs of people in our community and our world. We know that by healing and serving them, we heal and serve you. Thank you again for this time we've had to learn from one another and grow together in faith. We pray all these things in Jesus' name. Amen.

Session 4

THE GIFT OF LOVE

The Story of Marius and Cosette

PLANNING THE SESSION

Through this session's discussion and activities, participants will be encouraged to

- consider how God works in our lives through other people and how these people are miracles.
- reflect on the people who influence our ideas, passions, and beliefs.
- discuss how love and faith sometimes require us to take risks and leave old ideas and ways of living behind.
- explore what it means to be people of reconciliation and how we share in Christ's ministry of reconciliation.

PREPARATION

- Read and reflect on the fourth chapter of Matt Rawle's *The Grace of Les Misérables*.

- Read through this leader's guide session in its entirety to familiarize yourself with the material being covered.
- Read and reflect on the following Scriptures:

  ◊   Genesis 12:1-3
  ◊   Song of Solomon 8:6-7
  ◊   Mark 1:16-20
  ◊   John 15:12-14
  ◊   2 Corinthians 5:16-19
  ◊   Galatians 5:22-23

- Make sure that you have a whiteboard or large sheet of paper on which you can record group members' ideas.
- Have a Bible, paper for taking notes, and a pen or pencil available for every participant.

OPENING ACTIVITY AND PRAYER (5 MINUTES)

Opening Activity

As participants arrive, welcome them to this study. Ask participants to brainstorm their favorite love stories (from film, books, television, and so on). List these on a whiteboard or large sheet of paper. When everyone is present and has had a chance to contribute, discuss:

- What makes these stories and their characters so compelling?
- What, if anything, can we learn from the relationships portrayed in these stories?

Keep this list handy. You will return to it later in the session.

Opening Prayer

Lord, as we continue this study, we thank you for the gifts of love and relationships. We thank you for the story of Les Misérables, *and for what it teaches us about being people of love and reconciliation. Bless our time together that we can learn from Scripture, from story, and from one another. Amen.*

WATCH DVD SEGMENT (10 MINUTES)
STUDY AND DISCUSSION (35 MINUTES)

Cosette

Corresponds with "Cosette" in *The Grace of Les Misérables*, pages 84–87.

Read aloud or summarize for the group:

Cosette, Fantine's daughter, has a rough childhood. At a young age Fantine places her daughter in the care of the Thénardier family so that she can work in the factory. The Thénardiers exploit this arrangement, extorting Fantine for more money and abusing Cosette. Fantine later loses her factory job and resorts to extreme measures to make ends meet before dying of tuberculosis.

One Christmas Eve the Thénardiers send Cosette into the cold night to fetch water. While she is in the dark, terrified, Cosette meets Jean Valjean, the former mayor of her mother's town, and a man who'd promised Fantine that he'd make sure her daughter was cared for. Meeting Jean Valjean is a miracle for Cosette. He takes her in and frees her from the abusive Thénardiers. He gives her hope for a better future.

Of course, Cosette's life with Valjean isn't perfect. Because of his legal troubles, the pair spend a lot of time in hiding. Cosette hopes to experience the world, but Valjean is reluctant—and afraid—to let her go. Many of us can relate to Cosette and Valjean's relationship, either as a child or as a parent. We can probably identify people in our lives who loved us, cared for us, and made tremendous sacrifices for us but nonetheless made mistakes and didn't always know what was best.

For discussion:

- What people have been miracles in your life? Who has been there for you at exactly the right time?
- What other miraculous moments have made you the person you are today?
- Other than parents and guardians, who in your life has loved, cared for, and made sacrifices for you? How have you seen God at work in these people?

- If you are a parent, when have you made assumptions about what was best for your children that turned out to be wrong?
- Why, do you think, does God so often work through people who are flawed and prone to making mistakes?

Marius

Corresponds with "Marius" in *The Grace of Les Misérables*, pages 87–91.

Read aloud or summarize for the group:

Hugo's novel goes much deeper into his story. Following the death of Marius's mother, his maternal grandfather takes him in as a child. This grandfather is devoted to the new French monarchy and does not care for his son-in-law—Marius's father—who had served under Napoleon. Marius's grandfather does not allow him to spend time with his father, and Marius adopts his grandfather's politics.

Marius doesn't know much about his father until after his father's death. He learns that Napoleon had named his father a baron. This information turns Marius against the monarchy and in favor of the return of the empire. When he meets Enjolras, Marius turns even further away, rejecting the idea of restoring the empire and becoming a revolutionary.

The Marius we meet in the book is impressionable. He is passionate about French politics, but his allegiance shifts as he is influenced by different people. Many of us, if we're honest with ourselves, can probably relate. No matter how confident we are in our convictions, our families, our peers, and influential people in our culture affect our passions and beliefs. As followers of Christ, we should judge all ideas and influences against the truths and principles we adhere to.

For discussion:

- What persons have had the biggest impact on your beliefs, passions, and tastes?
- What made these persons so influential?
- Which of these persons turned out to be bad influences? Why?
- What core beliefs and principles do we, as Christians, adhere to?

- Read Galatians 5:22-23. How do these (or how *could* these) fruits of the Spirit influence what you believe in and invest your time in?
- What changes might you need to make to bring your ideas and passions in line with these fruits of the Spirit?

Finding Each Other

Corresponds with "Finding Each Other" in *The Grace of Les Misérables*, pages 91–94.

Read aloud or summarize for the group:

Marius grew up affluent under the care of his grandfather. But when he leaves home after a confrontation with his grandfather, he has little money to his name. While the freedom and hope of a new life is exciting, Marius struggles at first. After about six months on his own, Marius notices Cosette one day in the Luxembourg Gardens and is infatuated. Falling in love with someone he hardly knows is true to Marius's character. After all, this is a guy who went from monarchist to imperialist to revolutionary in a short period of time. At this point in the story, we have to wonder whether Marius's love for Cosette is true or if it is another passing obsession.

Marius would be able to relate to many people in Scripture. In Genesis God calls Abram and Sarai to leave their land and their family and to relocate to Canaan. The couple, who are already elderly, don't know what the future holds—and they deal with many trials and struggles—but they know that God has promised to bless them and their ancestors. When Jesus calls his first disciples, he asks them to leave behind their lives and jobs and to follow him. Leaving behind an established fishing business to follow an upstart traveling teacher would've seemed crazy to most people, but their decisions to join Jesus would change their lives and the world.

Scripture also speaks to the romantic love that Marius felt toward Cosette. Song of Solomon, a book in the Old Testament, is a poem between two people in love. But the love expressed in Song of Solomon isn't a "love at first sight"; it is a love grounded in loyalty and devotion. The two people in this poem truly know and care for one another. While Marius may one day feel this sort of loyalty and devotion toward Cosette, he is not there yet.

For discussion:

- When have you had an abrupt change in your life? How was this change frightening? How was it exciting?
- Read Genesis 12:1-3. What does God ask Abram and his family to do? What promises does God make to Abram and his family?
- If you were in Abram and Sarai's situation, how would you have responded to God? What questions would you have asked?
- Read Mark 1:16-20. Why, do you think, do these disciples leave everything and follow Jesus right away? What questions or concerns might they have had?
- Read Song of Solomon 8:6-7. What do these verses have to say about the love between the woman who is speaking and the man she loves? How is this love different from the infatuation that people sometimes feel for another person?

Love and Truth

Corresponds with "Love and Truth" in *The Grace of Les Misérables*, pages 94–98.

Read aloud or summarize for the group:

While Marius's love for Cosette begins as infatuation, their love grows as they exchange letters. Soon Jean Valjean discovers their correspondence and becomes upset, afraid that his adopted daughter—the one person he has ever truly loved—will leave him. He plans to move Cosette with him to England.

Devastated by the prospect of losing Cosette, Marius decides that he has nothing to lose and joins the insurgents at the barricades. Without Cosette, he feels that he has nothing to lose and acts with a reckless bravery. Marius is not alone at the barricades. Many of the would-be revolutionaries are not fighting for the cause as much as they are fighting for personal reasons.

Attitudes change when Gavroche is shot and killed while gathering munitions. His death rallies the revolutionaries; suddenly they have something to fight for. Marius goes beyond the barricade to retrieve Gavroche's body and is shot. Marius ends up critically wounded. Valjean must drag Marius through the sewers to get him to a safe place where he might have a chance at recovery.

For discussion:

- Read John 15:12-14. What does Jesus instruct his followers to do in these verses?
- What does it mean that Jesus calls us his friends in these verses?
- When have you taken a stand for a just cause for reasons that were selfish?
- What moments and experiences have inspired you to set aside self-interest and work for a greater cause?

The Greatest of These Is Love

Corresponds with "The Greatest of These Is Love" in *The Grace of Les Misérables*, pages 98–101.

Read aloud or summarize for the group:

Marius's story is a story of reconciliation. After Jean Valjean saves his life and drags him through the sewers, Marius recovers under the watch and care of his grandfather. (It is important to note that Marius is not aware that Valjean was the one who saved him because Valjean never tells him.) Marius and his grandfather had not parted on good terms, and his grandfather—a supporter of the monarchy—has no love for the insurrectionists. When Marius regains his health, he and his grandfather are able to set aside their political differences and reunite as a family. Marius asks his grandfather's permission to marry Cosette, and his grandfather eagerly gives his blessing.

Following Marius and Cosette's wedding, Valjean tells Marius the truth about his identity and his history as a thief and criminal. Repulsed by Valjean's dishonesty and criminal past, Marius gradually distances his new father-in-law from Cosette. Eventually Marius learns that Valjean was the one who had saved his life. This information convinces Marius to reconcile with his father-in-law, and Marius, Cosette, and Valjean finally are united as a family.

Les Misérables, as the title suggests, is a story of hardship and misery. But it's also a love story. Not a love story in the romantic comedy sense of the phrase, but a story that shows the enduring and redeeming power of love. Because of love, the protagonists in *Les Misérables* persevere through injustice, violence, poverty, abuse, and sickness until they ultimately find peace and reconciliation.

For discussion:

- When have you been reconciled with a friend or family member with whom you fell out of favor? What brought you back together?
- Read 2 Corinthians 5:16-19. What is the difference between recognizing people by "human standards" and seeing them as part of Christ's "new creation"?
- What, do you think, does it mean that Christ has entrusted us with his "message of reconciliation"?
- How has love given you hope, inspiration, or the will to persevere during a time of difficulty?

Activity: Love Stories, Revisited

Supplies: the list of love stories from the opening activity, a whiteboard or large sheet of paper, and markers

Refer back to the list of love stories you compiled during the opening activity. If you haven't already, add *Les Misérables* to the list.

Reflect on the qualities that make the relationships in these stories strong and successful. List these qualities on a whiteboard or large sheet of paper. The person who names each quality should say how that quality is present in one or more of the stories on your list. For example, if someone says, "loyalty," he or she should explain how the characters in one or more of the stories are loyal to each other.

Once you have a good list, go through the qualities you've named and discuss which of them apply to all healthy human relationships—not just the sort of romantic relationships portrayed in books and movies.

Discuss:

- What can you learn from the love stories we've discussed about showing love to all God's people?

Activity: Love in the Bible

Supplies: the list of love stories from the opening activity, a whiteboard or large sheet of paper, and markers

Say something like: "The Bible has all sorts of love stories, but most of them wouldn't make for a Netflix romantic comedy. They teach us about all sorts of love—love between family members, love between friends, love between strangers, and love between enemies."

Read aloud the stories below from Scripture. For each one, identify: (1) Who are the people "in love"? (2) What type of relationship is described? (3) What can we learn from this story that applies to our lives?

- Ruth 1:1-17
- 1 Samuel 19:1-3; 20:1-4, 24-34, 41-42
- Luke 10:25-37
- John 12:1-8
- 2 Timothy 1:3-8

CLOSING ACTIVITY AND PRAYER (10 MINUTES)

Closing Activity

Title a large sheet of paper, "What Christians can learn from the stories and relationships of Marius and Cosette." To close your time together, have each person list on the large sheet of paper one thing that he or she has learned about his or her faith from this session. Invite participants to explain what they wrote.

Closing Prayer

God of relationships and reconciliation, thank you for the stories that teach us about what it means to love one another as you have loved us. Open our eyes, ears, and minds to ways that we can be people of love and reconciliation in our families, in our communities, and in our world. Thank you again for this time we've had to learn from one another and grow together in faith. We pray all these things in Jesus' name. Amen.

Session 5

BUILDING THE BARRICADE

The Story of Les Amis

PLANNING THE SESSION

Through this session's discussion and activities, participants will be encouraged to

- consider what it means for Jesus to be king and what his kingdom looks like.
- reflect on which human leaders, institutions, and ideas compete for our loyalty.
- examine biblical accounts of Jesus' trial and what they teach us about Jesus' role as king.

PREPARATION

- Read and reflect on the fifth chapter of Matt Rawle's *The Grace of Les Misérables*.
- Read through this Youth Study Book's session in its entirety to familiarize yourself with the material being covered.

- Read and reflect on the following Scriptures:

    ◊ Luke 17:20-21
    ◊ Luke 22:32-38
    ◊ John 18:33-37
    ◊ John 19:1-14

- Make sure that you have a whiteboard or large sheet of paper on which you can record group members' ideas.
- Have a Bible, paper for taking notes, and a pen or pencil available for every participant.

OPENING ACTIVITY AND PRAYER (5 MINUTES)

Opening Activity

As participants arrive, welcome them to this study. The story of *Les Misérables* intersects with actual events that took place in France during the first half of the nineteenth century. Discuss these questions:

- What do you know about what was happening in France during the first half of the nineteenth century?
- What do you know about the French Revolution? (The French Revolution happened in 1789 but set the stage for many of the events that influence *Les Misérables*.)
- What do you know about Napoleon and his time as ruler of France?

As needed, explain: In the late 1700s in France, resentment toward the monarchy and nobility bubbled up until, in 1789, common folk stormed the Bastille fortress and started a revolution. Within a few years, the monarchy was abolished, a republic was established, and many in the former ruling class (including the king) had been executed.

The other European powers hoped to contain the revolution and to restore monarchy in France. Fights with powerful neighbors weakened and bankrupted the new French republic and enabled a military leader named Napoleon Bonaparte to gain popular support. Napoleon managed to get himself elected First Consul and established a constitution for the French Consulate. Some in France were unhappy that Napoleon had become so powerful, and he was able to use several failed assassination plots to his advantage. He expanded his power and, in 1804, became the emperor of France.

The French Empire under Napoleon expanded its reach, conquering territory in Spain, Italy, Germany, and other surrounding countries. Eventually a coalition led by Russia was able to defeat Napoleon, and the empire fell in 1814. Napoleon was replaced by a constitutional monarchy led by the Bourbons, the family that had ruled before the Revolution. This lasted until the July Revolution of 1830 that removed the Bourbons from power and replaced them with the house of Orleans. The new regime promised to make democratic reforms, but it soon became clear that little would change. Wealthy nobles still controlled France, often at the expense of everyone else. Two years later, a group of workers, students, and refugees organized and revolted. This is the 1832 uprising we encounter in *Les Misérables*.

Opening Prayer

Lord, as we continue this study, we thank you for the gift of grace. We thank you for the story of Les Misérables, *and for the questions it raises about where our loyalties lie and how we serve you first. Bless our time together that we can learn from Scripture, from story, and from one another. Amen.*

WATCH DVD SEGMENT (10 MINUTES)
STUDY AND DISCUSSION (35 MINUTES)
Fanning the Flames

Corresponds with "Fanning the Flames" in *The Grace of Les Misérables*, pages 104–108.

Read aloud or summarize for the group:

Though *Les Misérables* is fiction, the story is grounded in historical events. General Jean Maximilien Lamarque had served with distinction under Napoleon. Later in his life, he devoted himself to human rights, supporting freedom movements in Italy and Poland and speaking out against the constitutional monarchy in France. Victor Hugo, author of *Les Misérables*, portrays him as a hero to the poor. Lamarque died of cholera amid an epidemic in 1832. He had become a popular figure among students who were fighting for change, and his funeral procession drew such a large crowd that the government posted thousands of troops and erected barricades in and around Paris to keep the peace. Some shots are fired, there are some skirmishes, and lives are lost.

Rawle sees parallels between Lamarque's funeral procession in *Les Misérables* and Jesus' triumphal entry into Jerusalem in Scripture. Both events draw big crowds and make the authorities nervous. The people who are present for both processions have big ideas about what *could* happen but don't really know what *will* happen. The students waiting out the night in Paris after Lamarque's funeral, like Jesus' disciples at the Last Supper, break bread and drink wine together. And, like Jesus' disciples, they aren't really clear about what the next day will bring.

For discussion:

- Scripture gives us the impression that Jesus' disciples didn't really understand what was going to happen to Jesus on the day following the Last Supper. Read Matthew 26:26-29. What might the disciples have been thinking when Jesus, during the first Holy Communion, said, "I won't drink wine again until that day when I drink it in a new way with you in my Father's kingdom"?
- When have you been up all night because you were anxious about or eager for what would happen the next day? How did the following day live up to or fall short of your expectations?
- What events in recent history have sparked unrest and uprisings? What was so significant about these events?
- How should we, as Christians, respond during times of unrest and violence?
- How can we advocate for an important cause without resorting to violence? Are there ever situations when violence is necessary or inevitable? Why, or why not?

Who Should Sit on the Throne?

Corresponds with "Who Should Sit on the Throne?" in *The Grace of Les Misérables*, pages 108–11.

Read aloud or summarize for the group:

People in power tend to want to keep their power. And they don't look favorably on those who threaten their power. In *Les Misérables* we see the authorities in Paris strive to put down the 1832 uprising before it became another French Revolution. In Scripture we see Pontius Pilate give in to those calling for Jesus' death before they threaten the security of Jerusalem during the Passover. And the fact that Jesus was put to death on a cross suggests that Pilate and other leaders consider Jesus and his followers a threat to their power.

The students in *Les Misérables* want to start a revolution in Paris. They are tired of royals and nobles who look down on them and neglect the poor. But the young rebels lack the guns and numbers to take on the powerful government forces, and their revolution is unsuccessful.

Had Jesus and his followers led a similar insurrection in Jerusalem, it might have met the same end. But Jesus' revolution didn't involve overthrowing the government by force. When Jesus tells Pilate about his kingdom, Pilate assumes that he is making a political statement. But, as Jesus explains, his kingdom is not "from here." Jesus is a different kind of king, greater than any ruler who sits on a throne in Paris or Rome or anywhere else in the world.

For discussion:

- For what reasons might a group revolt against its rulers?
- Christians often call Jesus a king. What does it mean for Jesus to be a king?
- How is Jesus similar to earthly kings? How is he entirely different?
- Read John 18:33-37. What does Jesus say about his kingdom in these verses?
- What, do you think, does Pilate think of Jesus' answers? Why might he consider Jesus a threat?
- How does recognizing Jesus as your king affect how you live? How does it affect your attitude toward earthly leaders?

When Only Bloodshed Remains

Corresponds with "When Only Bloodshed Remains" in *The Grace of Les Misérables*, pages 111–14.

Read aloud or summarize for the group:

Javert, in *Les Misérables*, has no sympathy for criminals. He doesn't care about why they committed their crimes, he doesn't care about injustices that make it more likely for people to resort to crime, and he isn't really interested in their redemption. As we've seen before in this study, Javert doesn't understand concepts like grace and forgiveness.

Pilate in John's Gospel has a similar attitude. Pilate says twice that he finds no grounds to bring charges against Jesus. But he considers Jesus some sort of troublemaker and has no problem having Jesus whipped, humiliated, and executed to appease an angry crowd.

Jesus is the ultimate expression of God's grace. Through Jesus Christ we have hope for forgiveness and redemption. When we fail to reflect this grace, the result is apathy, resentment, and often violence.

For discussion:

- Read John 19:1-7. Why, do you think, did Pilate hand over Jesus to be beaten and mocked if he found "no grounds for a charge against him"?
- Read John 19:8-14. Why, do you think, is Pilate afraid (verse 8)?
- What excuses do we come up with to treat other people cruelly?
- What happens to our relationships and our communities when we fail to treat one another with grace and forgiveness?

We Always Choose Barabbas

Corresponds with "We Always Choose Barabbas" in *The Grace of Les Misérables*, pages 114–18.

Read aloud or summarize for the group:

We can see parallels between the factions in the Jewish world of Jesus' day and the people and groups we meet in *Les Misérables*. France in the early nineteenth century has wealthy and powerful nobles who help the monarchy maintain its power over the country's cities and towns. In first-century Judaism, the Sadducees worked closely with the Roman authorities and maintained the temple.

49

Javert, in *Les Misérables*, represents law enforcement. He is committed to following and upholding the law on a level that most are incapable of. The Pharisees of Jesus' day had similar feelings toward Jewish law. They expressed their faith by following every law to the letter.

The Essenes in the first-century Jewish world withdrew from society and focused on personal holiness. They had no interest in overthrowing the Roman government, but they also didn't care to participate in Roman culture. Jean Valjean spends much of *Les Misérables* hiding from the authorities, and he doesn't care to get involved with political matters. He is aware of injustice but struggles with whether or not he should fight against it.

The 1832 uprising is a key event in *Les Misérables* (and in nineteenth-century French history). Enjolras and the other student revolutionaries wanted a regime change and a new form of government in France. In Jesus' day, the Zealots had similar goals. They wanted the Roman authorities out of Galilee and Judea so that the land would again be under Jewish rule.

Prior to Jesus' crucifixion, Pilate gave the crowd a choice of releasing either Jesus or a man named Barabbas. Barabbas was a revolutionary, likely a Zealot. Jesus was harder to place. He had things in common with each of the groups, but he looked forward to a world where people weren't divided into factions but were united in their commitment to the well-being of all people. Sadly, in our sinful and broken world, we tend to define ourselves by what divides us.

For discussion:

- Which of the groups from Jesus' day—Sadducees, Pharisees, Essenes, or Zealots—do you most relate to? If you were alive in the first-century Jewish world, which group would you most likely have been a part of?
- Which person or group in *Les Misérables*—the nobles, the revolutionaries, Javert, Jean Valjean, Cosette, Fantine, or someone else—do you relate to most? Why?
- Read John 18:36. What, do you think, does Jesus mean when he says that his kingdom is not of this world?
- Read Luke 17:20-21. What, do you think, does Jesus mean when he says that God's kingdom is already among us? How is God's kingdom already present in our world today?

Tragedy

Corresponds with "Tragedy" in *The Grace of Les Misérables*, pages 118–20.

Read aloud or summarize for the group:

Late in the evening, while the revolutionaries are gathered by the barricades, the French National Guard attacks. It soon becomes clear that the rebels have neither the numbers nor the resources to resist the military. Sensing defeat, Enjolras instructs those who have children to retreat and return home.

Enjolras and the other rebels feel that they are fighting for a just cause. But their efforts fall short. Many others throughout history have met a similar fate. Others have been victorious on the battlefield but nonetheless have been scarred by what they experienced and have wondered if their efforts were worth the cost.

War and violence are inevitable in our broken, sinful world. But as Christians, we know the truth that the only blood that needed to be spilled was Jesus'. When Jesus is on the cross, with people jeering him and soldiers dividing up the clothes they'd taken from him, he says, "Father, forgive them, for they don't know what they're doing" (Luke 23:34). Jesus calls out to God to show us mercy as we continue to bring about suffering, tragedy, and violence.

In the musical, after the uprising Marius goes back to the pub where he and his friends had met to plan the insurrection. He expresses doubt about whether the revolt had been worth the lives that were lost, and he feels guilt about being one of the lucky survivors. But his story wasn't over. And the story of the French people wasn't over. And the story of humankind isn't over. God promises us that, through Christ, one day the violence will end and we will experience true peace and reconciliation.

For discussion:

- When have you, like Enjolras, had a moment when you realized that something you'd hoped for would not happen? How did you respond to this truth?
- When have you put a lot of time and effort into something, only to question whether the result was worth what you put into it?

- Read Luke 22:32-38. What, do you think, does Jesus mean when he says, "Father, forgive them, for they don't know what they're doing?" How do they not know what they're doing?
- What can we do to give people a glimpse of the peace and reconciliation that God promises?

Activity: *You Say You Want a Revolution*

Supplies: small sheets of paper or index cards and pens or pencils

Distribute small sheets of paper or index cards. Each person should write on the cards or slips about a time when they looked forward to an event they expected to change their lives, their community, or the world. Maybe they had put their hope in the election of a certain political leader, a particular law or policy going into effect, or the development of a new technology.

On their slips or cards participants also should answer the questions:

- What did you hope would happen?
- What actually happened?

Invite each participant to talk about what they'd looked forward to and to say how they answered the questions. Then discuss:

- Which of our examples were disappointments?
- Which were pleasant surprises?
- What are the dangers in putting our hope in human leaders, rules, and technologies?
- How would our lives and our expectations be different if we put our hopes entirely in God?

Activity: *Who Is Your Ruler?*

Supplies: a whiteboard or large sheet of paper and markers

Much of the unrest in France in the late eighteenth and early nineteenth centuries centered around the question of leadership. The 1832 rebellion was a reaction to the leadership of King Louis Philippe.

Leadership also was a key theme in Jesus' trial and execution. Pilate began his questioning of Jesus by asking, "Are you the king of the Jews?" (John 18:33). Jesus explained, "My kingdom doesn't originate from this world" (John 18:36).

As Christians, we look to Jesus as our king and know that his kingdom is greater than any nation or institution on earth. But we still find ourselves serving earthly kings and queens. We do this whenever our identity as a follower of Christ takes a back seat to our loyalty to other people or brands or institutions.

Brainstorm a list of the kings and queens we serve. This might include political leaders or parties; other influential persons; brands that influence our actions and choices; and activities that we are fully devoted to, sometimes at the expense of other people and commitments. Write these on a whiteboard or sheet of paper.

When you have a good list, discuss:

- Why are we loyal to these earthly rulers?
- How does our loyalty to these kings and queens affect our relationships with God and other people?
- How should our faith affect our priorities? What does it say about the people, institutions, and activities we're loyal to?
- How are our lives and relationships different when we are fully devoted to our relationship with Christ?

CLOSING ACTIVITY AND PRAYER (10 MINUTES)

Closing Activity

Title a large sheet of paper, "What Christians can learn from the story of the 1832 uprising." To close your time together, have each person list on the large sheet of paper one thing that he or she has learned about his or her faith from this session. Invite participants to explain what they wrote.

Closing Prayer

God of endurance, character, and hope, thank you for the stories that teach us about our loyalties and priorities and about the sacrifice you made on our behalf. Open our eyes, ears, and minds to ways that we can serve you faithfully and resist the temptation to serve earthly rulers. Thank you again for this time we've had to learn from one another and grow together in faith. We pray all these things in Jesus' name. Amen.

Session 6

THE BLESSED GARDEN
A Hopeful Vision

PLANNING THE SESSION

Through this session's discussion and activities, participants will be encouraged to

- consider the role that gardens play in *Les Misérables* and in Scripture.
- reflect on God's gift of sabbath rest and the importance of setting aside time for reflection and recovery.
- discuss ways that we cultivate and tend to our faith.
- examine how Christ has been present since Creation and will bring all things to fulfillment.

PREPARATION

- Read and reflect on the sixth chapter of Matt Rawle's *The Grace of Les Misérables*.
- Read through this Youth Study Book's session in its entirety to familiarize yourself with the material being covered.

- Read and reflect on the following Scriptures:
  - ◊ Genesis 1:28-31
  - ◊ Genesis 2:4-9
  - ◊ Leviticus 25:8-18
  - ◊ Matthew 26:36-50
  - ◊ Luke 5:15-16
  - ◊ Luke 6:1-11
  - ◊ Colossians 1:15-20
  - ◊ Revelation 21:1-4
  - ◊ Revelation 21:22-25
  - ◊ Revelation 22:1-5
- Make sure that you have a whiteboard or large sheet of paper on which you can record group members' ideas.
- Have a Bible, paper for taking notes, and a pen or pencil available for every participant.

OPENING ACTIVITY AND PRAYER (5 MINUTES)

Opening Activity

As participants arrive, welcome them to this study. Ask:

- What comes to mind when you think of a garden?

List ideas that people come up with on a whiteboard or large sheet of paper.

When most people are present, discuss:

- What ideas about or descriptions of gardens surprised you?
- What different types of gardens have we described?
- What are some famous gardens?
- Why, do you think, do we cultivate and maintain gardens? Other than gardens that provide food, what is the purpose of gardens?

Opening Prayer

Lord, as we begin the final session of this study, we thank you for the gifts of grace and peace. We thank you for the grace that you showed in the creation of all things, the grace that Jesus demonstrated through his arrest and death and resurrection, and the grace we see in your promise to make all things new. Bless our time together that we can learn from Scripture, from story, and from one another. Amen.

WATCH DVD SEGMENT (10 MINUTES)

STUDY AND DISCUSSION (35 MINUTES)

The Tale of Three Gardens

Corresponds with "The Tale of Three Gardens" in *The Grace of Les Misérables,* pages 122–26.

Read aloud or summarize for the group:

Gardens are a recurring element in *Les Misérables.* They are mentioned throughout the original novel, and much of the action takes place there. Gardens also play a major role in Scripture. The Bible opens in a garden when God places the first humans in a garden called Eden. As Scripture rises to its climax, we see Jesus praying in the garden of Gethsemane, preparing for his trial, death, and resurrection. And the Bible's grand resolution, in the final chapters of Revelation, also takes place in a garden. The garden in Revelation is portrayed as a new, restored Eden in the middle of a glorious New Jerusalem.

These gardens tell our story as God's people. In Eden, humankind lives with God in peace. But the humans in the garden succumb to pride and rupture our relationship with God. From this point on we see God in Scripture working to restore this relationship.

The ultimate expression of God's restorative grace is God living among us in the person of Jesus Christ. Jesus sacrifices himself to deliver us from sin and death. The night before he does, he prays in the garden of Gethsemane. Jesus' time in the garden is not pleasant. He agonizes about what he must do, but he understands that he must do God's will. After this prayer, Jesus is arrested.

In Revelation, the Bible's closing book, John describes the end of suffering and God bringing all things to fulfillment. He writes of a new heaven and new earth, the centerpiece of which is the "New Jerusalem," a gleaming paradise made of gold and precious gems. A river of "life-giving water" flows through the middle of the city. On either side of the river is a "tree of life"—a mini garden—that bears fruit every month. The "tree of life" is a callback to Eden and creation being brought in line with God's will.

For discussion:

- What other stories can you think of that have recurring elements, such as the gardens in *Les Misérables*? How do these elements affect the story?
- What recurring elements have framed your life's story? (Examples might include schools, restaurants, parks, and so forth.)
- Read Genesis 2:4-9. Why, do you think, is it significant that God places the first humans in a garden? What, if anything, does this say about God's will for humankind?
- Read Matthew 26:36-50. What does Jesus pray for in the garden of Gethsemane? How would you describe his mood?
- In what ways is Jesus betrayed in the garden?
- Read Revelation 21:1-4 and 22:1-5. What do these verses say about God's will for all of creation?
- What is the connection between these verses in Revelation and the description of Eden in Genesis 2?

Finding Rest

Corresponds with "Finding Rest" in *The Grace of Les Misérables*, pages 126–29.

Read aloud or summarize for the group:

The novel version of *Les Misérables* suggests that God is present in gardens. Toward the beginning of the story, we see M. Bienvenu, the clergyman who gives Jean Valjean hope for a better life, walking through his garden each evening to find sabbath rest. Spending time in the garden each evening is a spiritual practice for M. Bienvenu. It's a way he connects with God. We connect with God and open ourselves to God's grace through spiritual practices such as sabbath rest and reflection. We first encounter the idea of setting aside time for sabbath in the Bible's first chapter. When God gives the law to the Israelites, one of the first Ten Commandments is to remember the sabbath and treat it as holy; the Book of Leviticus even instructs the people to set aside a Sabbath year to allow the land to rest. While Jesus in the New Testament clashes with religious leaders over how to observe the Sabbath, he teaches that the Sabbath is a gift from God, and we see him withdraw from his work and take time for prayer and recovery.

There is nothing wrong with working hard, and there are Scriptures that speak to the value of hard work. But our work can become an obsession that has a negative effect on our relationships with God and with one another. Time for rest gives us the opportunity to connect with God and to grow closer to our brothers and sisters in Christ.

For discussion:

- Where do you like to go for rest and recovery?
- Read Luke 6:1-11. What do these stories teach us about how to observe the Sabbath?
- Read Luke 5:15-16. What can we learn about sabbath rest from Jesus' example?
- How do you observe the Sabbath? How do you use sabbath rest as an opportunity to connect with God and others?
- When is it difficult to make time for sabbath rest? What excuses do we make for not resting and reconnecting with God?

A Garden's Difficult Work

Corresponds with "A Garden's Difficult Work" in *The Grace of Les Misérables*, pages 130–33.

Read aloud or summarize for the group:

Plenty of people, like M. Bienvenu, find rest in gardens. But gardens don't arise out of nowhere. Planting a garden—especially one large enough for people to spend time in—is hard work. After the initial tilling and planting is done, the gardener must ensure that plants have proper amounts of water and sunlight and fertilizer, must trim trees and bushes, and must pick fruits and vegetables as they ripen.

When Jean Valjean and Cosette are on the run in Paris, they find refuge in a garden at a convent. The gardener is a man named Fauchelevent, whose life Valjean had saved earlier in the story. In addition to providing Valjean and Cosette lodging in the convent, Fauchelevent offers Valjean a job as assistant gardener.

As a gardener, Valjean's work involves sowing and pruning. Sowing involves preparing the soil and planting something new. Pruning involves getting rid of branches that are dying or no longer producing fruit. Both of these aspects of gardening describe our life as followers of Christ. God calls us to take on new challenges and embrace new opportunities so that we can reach more people with the love and message of Christ. But God also instructs us to consider what we don't need in our lives and to get rid of anything that is hurtful or destructive.

For discussion:

- What do you know about gardening? What experience have you had with it?
- Gardening involves planting and sowing—creating a space where new plants can grow and flourish. How do you plant and sow in your spiritual life? What do you do to grow closer to God or to create opportunities for others to grow in faith?
- Maintaining a garden requires the gardener to prune branches that don't bear fruit. How is pruning part of your spiritual life? What sorts of things have you given up or gotten rid of so that you could grow in faith?
- What sorts of changes could you make in the coming weeks or months to better tend to your faith life and relationships with God and others?

Cultivation of the Wild

Corresponds with "Cultivation of the Wild" in *The Grace of Les Misérables*, pages 133–36.

Read aloud or summarize for the group:

Most of the gardens we've discussed in this session have been cultivated. People have tilled the ground, fertilized the soil, planted seeds, watered plants, plucked weeds, and pruned branches. But sometimes people want to withdraw to a place that isn't neatly managed and maintained but that is wild and natural. Such is the garden at Valjean's home, late in the story, where Cosette and Marius express their love for each other.

While humans have invested countless dollars and hours into curating gardens, we've also put a great deal of effort into making sure that wild, natural spaces are cared for. We set aside land for parks, for national forests, and for wildlife preservation. Many people prefer taking time for rest and recreation in these wild areas instead of in gardens that have been trimmed and tamed.

Parks and wild areas don't require the same type of regular maintenance that gardens do, but they still need care and protection. When we are in these spaces, we get constant reminders to take our trash with us and to prevent forest fires. But we must consider how our day-to-day actions—even when we are in our homes and cars and places of work—affect the natural world. We must be mindful about how much trash we produce, how much we make use of water and other resources, and what we put into our air. The wild spaces in our world not only provide places for us to get away but also serve as an example of God's pure, unspoiled creation and help sustain life on earth.

For discussion:

- What wild, natural areas have you enjoyed spending time in? What draws you to these places?
- What can we learn about God from the wild, unspoiled places on our planet?
- Read Genesis 1:28-31. What, do you think, does it mean that God told humankind to "fill the earth and master it" (verse 28)? How do we "master" our world? What do these verses tell us about our responsibility toward God's creation?
- What can we do on a daily basis to protect and care for the natural world?
- What does caring for the natural world have to do with our relationship with God?

God Is Still at Work

Corresponds with "God Is Still at Work" in *The Grace of Les Misérables*, pages 136–39.

Read aloud or summarize for the group:

Rawle writes, "Hugo means to show that the gardens throughout *Les Misérables* represent the different aspects of grace. Sometimes grace offers peace. Sometimes offering grace takes great work. Sometimes grace is wild and unexpected." We encounter gardens and grace early in Hugo's story, and these elements recur until the end.

We've already looked at how gardens tell the story of God's grace in Scripture: God places the first humans in a garden; Jesus spends time in a garden before his death and resurrection; the vision of a new heaven and earth in Revelation has a garden at its center. What we don't always recognize is that Christ is present throughout this story of grace.

Too often we confine Christ's story to the four Gospels. But John's Gospel begins by telling us that Christ is the Word of God and has been present since the beginning of creation. "Everything came into being through the Word,/and without the Word/nothing came into being" (John 1:3). In other words, Jesus was involved in creation and the life of God's people long before he lived on earth as a human being. In Revelation, the Bible's final book, we see Christ as the Lamb of God who brings all things to fulfillment. The story of humankind, and of God's love and grace, is the story of Christ.

For discussion:

- God's grace brings us peace. When have you experienced God's peace?
- Rawle says that offering God's grace sometimes takes "great work." When have you found it difficult to show God's grace to someone?
- God's grace can be wild and unexpected. When have you experienced God's unpredictable grace? When have you found grace where you least expected it?
- Read Colossians 1:15-20. What do these verses tell us about Christ and his role in God's story?

- Read Revelation 21:22-25. What do these verses tell us about the role that Christ (the Lamb) will play in God's new heaven and new earth?

Activity: Hit Reset

Supplies: Bibles

Ask participants who play video games:

- How do you decide when it's time to give up on the game you're playing, hit reset, and start over?

Ask all participants:

- When in your life (aside from times you were playing video games) have you wanted to hit reset and start over?

Say something like: "In this session, we considered the time M. Bienvenu spent in the garden and discussed the importance of sabbath rest. God commanded the Israelites to not only set aside a sabbath day but also a sabbath year. During the sabbath year, the people were to plant no crops and allow the land to rest. God went one step further: after every seventh sabbath year, God commanded the Israelites to observe a Jubilee year."

Read Leviticus 25:8-18. Discuss:

- What happens during the Jubilee year?
- How was the Jubilee year a way of hitting "reset"?
- How would observing a Jubilee every fifty years affect what people do during the other forty-nine years?
- Why, do you think, did God command the people to observe this Jubilee year?

Challenge participants to imagine that a Jubilee year is coming up next year. Discuss:

- What, do you think, would change for the better?
- What, do you think, would change for the worse?
- How might the Jubilee offer people hope?
- What fears would you have about the Jubilee?

Following this discussion, have each participant think of one way they can hit "reset" in their lives without waiting for a Jubilee year. This may involve refocusing their attention on something that used to be a priority but that they lost track of. It may involve starting over on a relationship with a friend or family member.

Participants should pair off and discuss with their partners the ideas they came up with.

Activity: *Plant a Garden*

Supplies: Paper, pens or pencils, a whiteboard or large sheet of paper, and markers

Divide participants into teams of three or four. Challenge each team to plan out a garden that is twenty feet long and thirty feet wide. Teams can place whatever they want in the garden—flowers, vegetables, trees, bushes, decorative rocks, and so forth—but they can spend only $100. Teams will need to access the Internet on phones or other devices to find prices for plants, seeds, saplings, and decorations. (For the purpose of this activity, the $100 doesn't need to cover the cost of soil, fertilizer, or tools.)

Give teams about five minutes to come up with what they'll put in their garden and to sketch a basic layout.

When they have a pretty good idea of what their garden will look like, have the teams come up with a list of tasks and responsibilities that will be required to maintain the garden (watering, weeding, pruning, picking, and so forth).

Invite each team to present its plan and the tasks required to maintain its garden.

Then discuss:

- What difficult decisions did you have to make about which plants and features to include in your garden? How are these decisions similar to those you've had to make about using money and resources individually or as part of a family?
- As a part of this activity, you had to create a list of tasks for maintaining your garden. What if you were to make a list of tasks for maintaining your faith? What would you include?

Challenge participants to brainstorm ways to tend and maintain their faith. List their ideas on a whiteboard or large sheet of paper. Encourage each person to commit to following through on one or more of these ideas in the weeks and months ahead.

CLOSING ACTIVITY AND PRAYER (10 MINUTES)

Closing Activity

Title a large sheet of paper, "What Christians can learn from the gardens in *Les Misérables* and in Scripture." To close your time together, have each person list on the large sheet of paper one thing that he or she has learned about his or her faith from this session. Invite participants to explain what they wrote.

Closing Prayer

God of grace and gardens, thank you for the blessed places in our world where we can find peace and rest and appreciate the magnificence of your creation. Open our eyes, ears, and minds to ways that we can be people of love, grace, and peace throughout your world. Thank you again for this time we've had to learn from one another and grow together in faith over the past several weeks. We pray all these things in Jesus' name. Amen.

CPSIA information can be obtained
at www.ICGtesting.com
Printed in the USA
LVHW082107251019
635274LV00007B/4/P